SOCCER

Pat Rediger

Weigl Publishers Inc.

Published by Weigl Publishers Inc.

123 South Broad Street, Box 227

Mankato, MN 56002

USA

Library of Congress Cataloging-in-Publication Data available upon request from the publisher.

Fax: (507) 388-2746 for the attention of the Publishing Records Department

ISBN 1-930954-10-7

Printed in the United States of America

3 4 5 6 7 8 9 05 04 03

Project Coordinator

Rennay Craats

Layout and Design

Warren Clark

Copy Editor

Heather Kissock

Photograph credits

Cover: EyeWire; Title: Visuals Unlimited (E. Webber); Contents: Reuters/ArchivePhotos (Robert Pratta); Archive Photos/Hulton-Getty: page 4, 16L; Corel Corporation: page 20L; EyeWire: page 12T, 13L,15T; Globe Photos: 7L (John Barrett), 16R (Jim Anderson), 18L (John Barrett), 18R (Dave Chancellor); Monique de St. Croix: pages 7R, 10L, 10R, 20R, 21L; National Soccer Hall of Fame: pages 17L, 17R; Newsport Photography Inc: 6 (William R. Sallaz),11L (Dan Helms), 19R (Dan Helms); Reuters/Archive Photos: 5R (Mike Brown), 11R (Robert Pratta), 14L (Gustau Nacarino), 14R (Zoraida Diaz), 22 (Mike Blake), 23L (Arnd Wiegmann); Tempsport/NewsportPhotography Inc: 12B (D. Iundt), 19L (Christian Liewig); Visuals Unlimited: pages 5L (H.Q. Stevens), 8 (Bill Kamin), 13R (E. Webber), 15B (E. Webber), 21R (Mark E. Gibson), 23R (Joe McDonald).

Every reasonable effort has been made to trace ownership and to obtain permission to reprint copyright material. The publishers would be pleased to have any errors or omissions brought to their attention so that they may be corrected in subsequent printings.

Contents

What is Soccer?

It is believed that soccer began in China in 2500 BC. Back then, the ball was made of animal skins and the players kicked it through a hole in a net. Soccer was played to celebrate the **emperor's** birthday. It was also played as a way to keep soldiers in shape.

Native Americans also played a similar game called pascuckuakohowog. This word means "they gather to play ball with the foot." They played on beaches, and the nets were about one mile apart. Sometimes 1,000 people played at a time. They could only tell their teammate by the paint and jewelry they wore. The games often lasted more than a day and ended with a feast.

Soccer has attracted enthusiastic fans since the early 1900s.

The soccer game played today came from England, where it is called football. It is hard to know exactly when people started playing the game there. New soccer rules were written in 1863, and they are the basis for what we play today.

Millions of people in more than 140 countries play soccer.

Soccer is a great game because it can be played almost anywhere. All that is needed is a level patch of ground, a ball, and two teams. The players handle the ball mainly with their feet. To score, players kick the ball into the other team's net. The team with the most number of **goals** at the end of the game wins.

Professional players develop incredible footwork and ball-handling skills.

CHECK IT OUT

To learn more about the history of soccer and more, surf over to

www.planet-soccer.com

What You Need

Soccer players do not need a lot of equipment to start playing. All they really need is a ball, a pair of shoes, and comfortable clothing.

Goalkeepers often wear pants, soft pads, gloves, and other protective equipment. Many goalkeepers wear the number one on their jerseys. Their uniform is a different color from all the other players on their team.

Players often wear shin pads to protect their legs.

Players wear **cleats** to play soccer. These shoes have pieces of plastic on the bottoms for better grip. There are rules about the size and shape of the cleats on soccer shoes. If they are too long, they could hurt another player.

There are hundreds of different kinds of soccer balls in use today. Soccer balls are round, made of leather, and bounce well. Balls must be 27 to 28 inches around. This is smaller than a basketball but larger than a volleyball. Soccer balls weigh between 14 and 16 ounces.

Players wear matching uniforms. They often have a large number on the back of their jerseys and a smaller one on the front.

During a soccer game, players may be asked to take off items that could hurt another player. These items include hard helmets, watches, or rings. Casts or braces must be wrapped so that no hard part of metal shows.

The same ball is used for the entire game unless the ball is defective.

Players wear loose shorts. They are comfortable and do not get in the way of running or kicking the ball.

The Playing Field

A soccer field, which is also called a pitch, can vary in size, but it is always rectangular. It can be no more than 130 yards by 100 yards.

The goal posts are 8 yards wide and 8 feet high. The **crossbars** around the goal are usually made of wood or metal. The goal area itself is 20 yards by 6 yards. Goal kicks are taken from anywhere in this area. The **penalty** area is in front of each goal. Only the goaltender is allowed to use his or her hands here.

Thirty-two countries compete for the world championships. The stadiums hold between 35,000 and 105,000 cheering fans.

CHECK IT OUT

To explore soccer links, turn to

www.reddingcal.com/ISKA/ISKA.html

The corner flags sit on posts. They are at least 5 feet high and are placed in each corner. Flags are also placed halfway down the field on both sides. The corner area extends out from the corner flag. The ball is placed here for a corner kick.

The center circle is 10 yards in **radius**. This circle keeps one team away from the ball when the other team takes the **kickoff**.

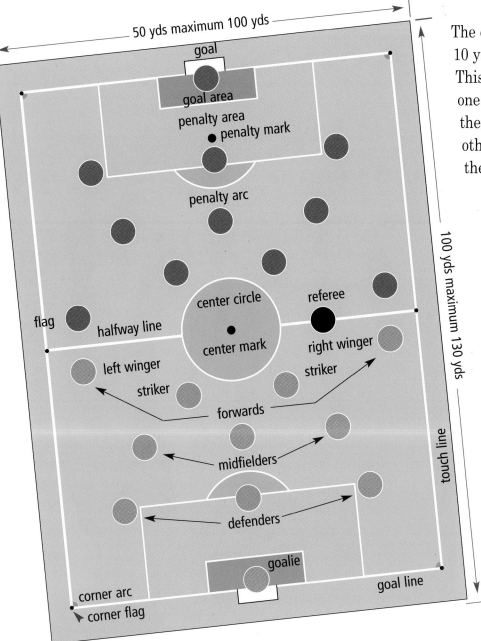

50 yds maximum 100 yds

goal

goal area

penalty area

penalty mark

penalty arc

center circle

referee

center mark

right winger

flag

halfway line

left winger

striker

striker

forwards

midfielders

defenders

goalie

corner arc

corner flag

goal line

touch line

100 yds maximum 130 yds

Rules of the Pitch

A soccer match lasts two periods of forty-five minutes. A goal is scored when the ball passes over the **goal line** between the goal posts. If the ball goes out of bounds, it is thrown in from that spot. The team that touches the ball last before it goes out of bounds loses **possession** of the ball. The other team throws it in.

During a throw-in, both feet must be on the ground. The player must throw the ball with two hands over his or her head.

A corner kick takes place when a ball goes out of bounds at the goal line, and the last one to touch it was a member of the defending team. A member of the attacking, or offensive, team puts the ball back into play. The ball is kicked from the quarter circle in the corner of the field.

When a free kick is taken, all players from the opposing team must stand 10 yards away. The opposing team can move toward the ball after it is kicked.

A goal kick occurs after the ball passes over the goal line and the last one to touch it was a member of the **attacking** team. A member of the defending team puts the ball back into play. The ball is kicked from inside the goal area. It must pass outside the penalty area before another player can touch it.

It is against the rules to kick or trip another player. Players also cannot hold or push other players. The ball cannot be handled with the player's hands or arms. Goalkeepers, however, can use their hands to block shots.

If these rules are broken, the ball is handed over to the other team. If the rules are broken again and again, the referee can penalize the player or the team. The referee can stop the game at any time if a **foul** has occurred. The referee may award the other team a penalty kick if a player breaks the rules. His or her decisions are final.

The linespeople help the referee. They determine when the ball is out of play. They also show which side can take a corner kick, goal kick, or throw-in.

Players are allowed to use their bodies against the player with the ball, but they cannot push or hold on to other players on the field.

Positions

There are several positions on a soccer team. The goalkeeper's job is to block the other team's shots on the net. Goalkeepers can use their hands with the ball only inside the penalty area. If they leave this area, they are treated like any other player and must use their feet to move the ball.

Defenders help their goalkeeper stop the other team from scoring. It is their job to prevent the other team's players from shooting at the goal at all. Defenders help block shots and get the ball away from the other team.

Different types of defenders play in different parts of the field. Fullbacks play down the sides. Centers play mainly in the area in front of the goal. Sometimes a team will have a sweeper who goes where she or he is most needed.

Any player on the team can substitute for the goalkeeper as long as the referee is informed.

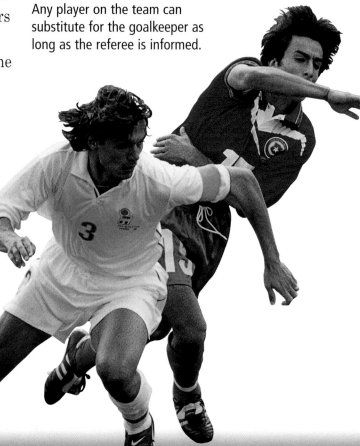

Defenders are sometimes called fullbacks. They take the ball from the other team and pass it to their teammates so they can score.

Midfielders move the ball mainly from the defenders to the forwards. Their job is to gain control of the ball when it is in the middle of the field. When the other team has the ball, midfielders try to get it back. When their own team has the ball, they try to set up plays to help the team score.

Teams usually have between two and five midfielders. A flank midfield player plays down the sides of the field. A central midfield player tries to score when attacking and tries to prevent a goal when defending.

Attackers, or forwards, try to score goals. Teams use anywhere from one to four players in this position. They must be able to pass well and control the ball. Attackers can kick the ball hard and right on target.

Soccer players use their heads in games! Heading allows players to pass or shoot a ball that is in the air.

Soccer games are usually low scoring. Scoring just one goal can be the difference between a win or a loss.

CHECK IT OUT

Become an expert on soccer by checking out

www.soccerclub.com

Leagues

Most children begin playing soccer in local leagues. This is where they learn how to play the sport. Those players who work hard can eventually play for college or university teams or the national teams. There are six men's national teams: World Cup, indoor, university, Olympic, and under seventeen years old. There are two women's national teams: World Cup/Olympic and under twenty years old.

World Cup soccer is a great event to watch. Each country fields its best players in hopes of winning the cup.

The European Cup takes place every four years, just like the World Cup.

The best players from universities and high schools are chosen to play for the national teams. They compete against players from other countries. The biggest tournament for national teams is the World Cup. The first World Cup tournament was held in 1930. Every country in the world that plays soccer competes in this tournament.

Winning any competition is a great accomplishment.

College teams are an excellent place to learn from experienced players and coaches.

Those who compete for the national teams are not paid. There are leagues for players who want to earn money. For example, Major League Soccer has twelve professional teams playing throughout the United States.

CHECK IT OUT

Follow your favorite players and teams at

www.wspsoccer.com

Superstars of the Sport

Soccer has had many fantastic players in its history. Many of these have made children want to play the game, too.

BOBBY CHARLTON

TEAM:
Manchester United

Career Facts:

- Bobby played forward for Manchester for twenty years. Upon his retirement, Bobby had scored 245 goals and only had one foul for delaying a free kick.
- In 1966, Bobby was voted the soccer player of the year.
- In 1958, Bobby survived a plane crash that killed twenty-three people, including eight soccer players.
- In 1994, Bobby was knighted for his services as an ambassador to soccer.
- Bobby led Manchester United to many victories, including the World Cup and the European Cup.

PELE

TEAM:
Brazilian National Team

Career Facts:

- Pele's first job was shining shoes.
- At the age of fifteen, Pele was invited to play for the Santos Futebol Club in Sao Paulo.
- When Pele was sixteen, he joined the Brazilian National Team.
- In his career, Pele played in fourteen World Cups and scored twelve goals in those competitions.
- In 1971, Pele joined the New York Cosmos to help make the game more popular in North America.

BILLY GONSALVES

TEAM:
Newark Football Club

Career Facts:

- Billy was known as the "**Babe Ruth**" of soccer.
- Billy played on several professional soccer teams in the United States, including Brooklyn Hispano, New Bedford Whalers, and Boston Wonder Workers.
- In the 1930s, Billy was one of only a handful of Americans who were good enough to play soccer in Europe.
- Billy won eight National Challenge Cup championships. This was the top American award in soccer during this time.

ALFREDA INGLEHART

POSITION:
Instructor

Career Facts:

- Alfreda was not a soccer player. She did, however, teach more than twelve hundred boys to play soccer.
- Alfreda helped make soccer popular in the United States.
- Many of Alfreda's students went on to become professional soccer players.
- In 1951, Alfreda was the first woman named to the National Soccer Hall of Fame.

Superstars of Today

The stars of today are thrilling fans and attracting more attention to soccer.

MIA HAMM

TEAM:
United States
National Soccer Team

Career Facts:

- At fifteen years old, Mia was the youngest player to play with the United States National Soccer team.
- In 1995 and 1997, Mia was named the Women's World Cup Most Valuable Player.
- Mia was named U.S. Soccer's Female Athlete of the Year from 1994 to 1998.
- Mia established a foundation to raise money for **bone marrow** research. Her brother had died of a rare blood disorder and had trouble receiving a bone marrow transplant.

DWIGHT YORKE

TEAM:
Manchester United

Career Facts:

- Dwight joined his high school soccer team. The national team coach spotted him and invited him to play in a game against England.
- In 1989, Dwight joined the Aston Villa team in Birmingham, England. He became the club's top scorer and led them to many successes.
- After nine years, Dwight was signed by Manchester United. Dwight led United in scoring and was named the top player in the league.
- Dwight is loved in his home country and a song has been written about him called "The Duke of Manchester."

PAOLO MALDINI

TEAM:
AC Milan

Career Fact:

- Paolo's father was a great soccer player and was captain of the AC Milan team in Italy.
- Paolo played several different positions in school before becoming a defender.
- Paolo played his first game for AC Milan in 1985. He was only sixteen years old.
- In 1988, Paolo was named to the Italian National Team.
- In 1994, Paolo became the captain of the Italian team and was named World Soccer's Player of the Year.
- Paolo became captain of AC Milan in 1998.

KASEY KELLER

TEAM:
United States
National Team

Career Facts:

- In 1994, Kasey played for Leicester, a top European team.
- Kasey started in more than three hundred professional games in Europe. That is more than twice as many as any other American player.
- Kasey led the United States National Team to win the 1998 Gold Cup against Brazil.
- Kasey was the starting goalkeeper for the United States World Cup team in 1998.

Staying Healthy

Just like you cannot run a car without fuel, you cannot play a good game of soccer without healthy food. Good **nutrition** is the key to keeping players at the top of their game.

Players often eat a variety of **carbohydrates** before they play. This means eating bread, raisins, watermelon, carrots, most types of cereals, spaghetti, bananas, and pineapple. They provide extra fuel for muscles during the game. These foods give players more energy on the field. A balanced diet of the major food groups is also important. Fruits and vegetables, along with breads and cereals, milk products, and meats, help keep people healthy. Drinking a lot of water every day also helps keep people running well.

There are many ways to train to become a better soccer player. Soccer players are always on the run, so they need to have strong hearts as well as muscles. Players often practice running while controlling the ball with their feet. They also practice running backwards without crashing into other players. Leg strength is important, and jumping, lunging, and stretching exercises help make players' leg muscles stronger.

During practice, players work on controlling the ball to help improve their skills.

Stretching before and after a game helps prevent injury.

CHECK IT OUT

Learn more about staying healthy for soccer by surfing over to

www.usysa.org

Soccer Brain Teasers

Test your knowledge of soccer by answering these soccer brain teasers!

Q Why did the 1974 World Cup Final not start on time?

A The officials forgot to put the flags in place.

Q When were shin guards first used?

A They were used for the first time in 1874.

Q When did the United States soccer team first play against another country?

A On November 28, 1885, the United States played against Canada. The Canadians won 1-0.

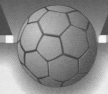

Q Why did India choose not to play in the 1950 World Cup?

A The team was not allowed to play in bare feet.

Q How many miles do soccer players run during a game?

A They often run about six or seven miles.

Q What sport is the national sport of the most countries in the world?

A Soccer. It is the national sport of countries ranging from Brazil and North Korea to Italy and England.

Glossary

attacking: offensive; having the ball and trying to score goals

Babe Ruth: a former home run champion in major league baseball

bone marrow: the material found inside people s bones

carbohydrates: foods that have materials that are good for building muscles and providing energy

cleats: shoes with hard plastic on the bottoms; they help players get a better grip on the grass when they run

crossbars: the three poles that make up the goal

emperor: the ruler of an empire

foul: when a player breaks one of the rules

goal: when a ball passes over the goal line between the goal posts

goal line: the line across the field that acts as the boundary

kickoff: a kick that puts a ball into play from the center line at the start of a quarter or after a goal has been scored

nutrition: foods that make up a good diet

penalty: punishment for breaking a rule or law

possession: having control of the ball; it changes from team to team many times throughout a game

radius: a straight line out from the center of a circle that reaches to the edge

Index

DATE DUE